Great Historic Debates and Speeches™

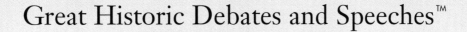

PATRICK HENRY'S LIBERTY OR DEATH SPEECH

A PRIMARY SOURCE INVESTIGATION

Jesse Jarnow

rosen central
Primary Source™

The Rosen Publishing Group, Inc., New York

Published in 2005 by The Rosen Publishing Group, Inc.
29 East 21st Street, New York, NY 10010

Library of Congress Cataloging-in-Publication Data

Jarnow, Jesse.
Patrick Henry's liberty or death speech : a primary source investigation / By Jesse Jarnow. — 1st ed.
    p. cm. — (Great historic debates and speeches)
Includes bibliographical references and index.
ISBN 1-4042-0152-1 (library binding)
1. Henry, Patrick, 1736–1799—Juvenile literature. 2. Legislators—United States—Biography—Juvenile literature. 3. United States. Continental Congress—Biography—Juvenile literature. 4. Virginia—Politics and government—1775–1783—Juvenile literature. 5. United States—Politics and government—1775–1783—Juvenile literature. 6. Henry, Patrick, 1736–1799—Oratory—Juvenile literature. 7. Speeches, addresses, etc., American—History and criticism—Juvenile literature.
I. Title. II. Series.
E302.6.H5J37 2005
973.3'092—dc22

                                                                2004001441

Manufactured in the United States of America

Cover images: Left: Painting of Patrick Henry by George Bagby Matthews, circa 1891. Right: Currier & Ives lithograph depicting the Liberty or Death speech.

CONTENTS

Patrick Henry was a natural leader and a moving speaker. His Liberty or Death speech inspired American freedom fighters during the Revolutionary War. He also exercised significant influence on the development of the United States in the postwar years.

This lithograph depicts Patrick Henry delivering his most famous speech at the second Virginia Convention in 1775. His concluding statement—"Give me liberty or give me death!"—became the battle cry of the Revolutionary War.

INTRODUCTION

March 23, 1775. The church was packed to the rafters. Men were crammed into the pews. Though the weather outside was bitterly cold, the windows were open and a chilly breeze relieved the stuffiness. People stood outside and gazed in at the delegates. The men had come from all over the colony of Virginia. Though they had been meeting for three days, their energy was little diminished. They were discussing an important issue: whether to rebel against England.

Most agreed that it was necessary. Talk of a rebellion had been brewing for some time. It had been festering for the past several years, as Britain levied a series of taxes on its American colonies. Britain imposed laws the colonists regarded as unfair. The Americans were upset. They wished to govern themselves. They longed for their own freedom. These questions remained: When? How?

In Virginia, as throughout the colonies, men met in conventions to discuss these questions. They rode across Virginia to Richmond to meet at the Henrico Parish Church (also known as St. Johns Church). Virginia was home to many of the colonies' finest politicians. Thomas Jefferson hailed from there, as did General George Washington. But there was one speaker more eagerly awaited than both of these great men. He was Patrick Henry.

Patrick Henry believed it was time for a revolution. When he rose to speak, he looked out on the crowd. He knew most of the men in the audience. He looked into their eyes and spoke. His speech built and rose. His hands cut shapes in the air. Theatrical flourishes punctuated his every remark, and the audience hung on every word. The delivery grew more intense as he urged the colonies to fight.

Henry raised his arms to the ceiling of the church. "I know not what course others may take," he said, his voice booming, practically shouting, "but as for me, give me liberty or give me death." Patrick Henry's speech provided the catchphrase of the American Revolution and framed a notion of liberty that stands today as a cornerstone of American democracy.

⊹═ CHAPTER 1 ═⊹

THE MAKINGS OF A REBEL LEADER

Hanover County, Virginia, was not a bad place to grow up in the early to mid-eighteenth century. When Patrick Henry was born in 1736, it was a land of many prospects. His father, John, had migrated from Scotland around 1718, hoping for a fresh start. Like the other British colonies on the North American continent, Virginia was full of promise. Compared to the increasingly overpopulated byways of Europe, the space of the colonies was seemingly endless. It was also rugged and uncultivated.

The colonies were officially under the control of the British Empire. However, life in the colonies bore little resemblance to life in England. It was relatively backward. There were no huge cities, and there were few outlets for cultural expression. There was untamed wilderness everywhere. Also, the social order was less established in comparison to England's. To many, there was nothing but untapped potential. To John Henry and others like him, America offered a new way of life. If one opportunity didn't work out, a person could simply seek out another.

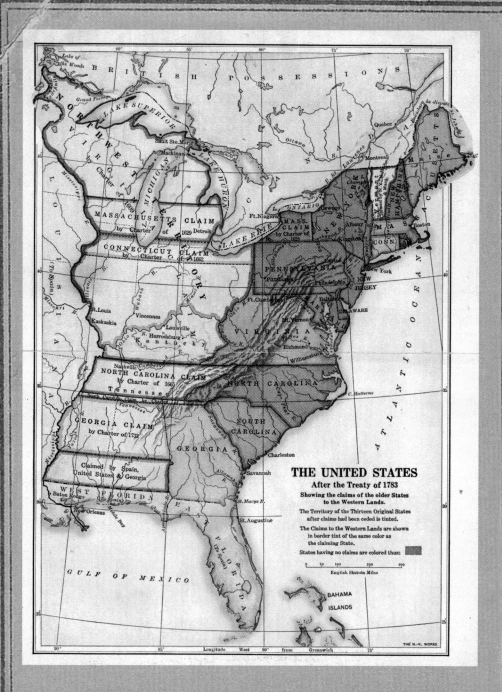

THE UNITED STATES

After the Treaty of 1783

Showing the claims of the older States
to the Western Lands.

The Territory of the Thirteen Original States
after claims had been ceded is tinted.

The Claims to the Western Lands are shown
in border tint of the same color as
the claiming State.

States having no claims are colored thus:

This map shows the thirteen American colonies at the time of the American Revolution. They were, in the order in which they were founded, Virginia, Massachusetts, Maryland, Rhode Island, Connecticut, Delaware, New Hampshire, North Carolina , South Carolina, New Jersey, New York, Pennsylvania, and Georgia.

After receiving a land grant, John Henry tried his hand at farming, to little success. In the 1730s, he got involved in a scheme to build a bridge across the Pamunkey River in Virginia. He invested in land on the other side, a town that would be known as Newcastle. Given its location on the river, investors hoped that it would grow into a city, possibly even a new capital. The plan didn't succeed. Soon, John Henry was farming again. With the optimism of a new American, he named his estate Mount Brilliant.

John schooled his children at home. Young Patrick received a basic classical education, learning some Latin and Greek, as well as other rudiments. With eight other children to raise, John struggled to make ends meet.

Early Influences

When Patrick was a child, Hanover County was in the grip of a religious revival. Itinerant Presbyterian and Baptist preachers passed through with frequency. Patrick's grandfather, Isaac Winston, was one of the first to be won over by these preachers. Though religious tolerance was practiced elsewhere in the colonies, it was harder to come by in backwoods Virginia. Most people there subscribed to the beliefs of the Anglican church, which was the Church of England. To them, doing otherwise was blasphemy (being disrespectful to God). Instead of attending an Anglican church, Winston and others participated in private Bible reading groups. Winston hosted traveling preachers in his home. He was persecuted for it. He had to pay fines to the local government, which regarded the practice of a non-Anglican faith as a disturbance of the peace.

Nonetheless, the preachers kept coming. In 1745, George Whitefield, the most famous of the revivalists, came through Hanover

Born in New Castle County in Delaware, Reverend Samuel Davies moved to Hanover County, Virginia, in 1747 as an evangelist when he was twenty-four years old. A powerful orator, he preached to thousands, including slaves, throughout the county. He founded five churches and later served as president of the College of New Jersey (now Princeton University).

County. Young Patrick watched him with interest. Two years later, Reverend Samuel Davies, a Presbyterian, moved to Hanover County. Though less famous than Whitefield, he would have a much greater influence on Patrick. Sarah Henry, Patrick's mother, took him to see Davies speak many times.

Davies was a masterful orator. He spoke with conviction. His words soared from his mouth and resounded through the church. Davies had a masterful control of his voice. He brought it from a delicate whisper to booming heights. Depending on his sermon, he could sound frightened, angry, or even like he was singing.

During the carriage rides home, Sarah would make Patrick repeat Davies's sermons. Soon, he was able to imitate Davies's voice. Though Patrick was never religiously converted by Davies, he found him a remarkable inspiration. Later, he would call Davies the greatest speaker he had ever seen. To join a non-Anglican church was an act of protest against the old ways. In being so profoundly influenced by Davies, Patrick was inherently anti-British from a young age.

Just as much as Patrick was shaped by his experiences seeing Reverend Davies, he was also shaped by experiences with his father. John Henry was quite active in the local Anglican church. But the local church meant far more than religion. Men would arrive early and discuss business and politics in the churchyard. They talked about the current prices of various crops. They bet on horse races and cockfights. After the service, Patrick and his father would spend the day in town. Patrick vastly enjoyed these Sundays. They gave Patrick his first taste of a life in which politics, business, and religion were combined. These experiences deeply shaped the kind of politician Patrick would one day become.

A Call to Law

Before that happened, though, Patrick tried his hand at a variety of occupations that contributed to his personality. Although he was a smart young man, his father couldn't afford to send him to Europe for school (as he would have liked) or even to Williamsburg, where the College of William and Mary had been established. Instead, he arranged for Patrick to apprentice for a shopkeeper in Newcastle. After several months, John Henry purchased goods on credit and helped Patrick and his brother William establish a store. It was a small store. It didn't do well and soon failed. Then it was on to another venture.

In 1754, Patrick Henry married Sarah Sallie Shelton, the daughter of John Shelton, a wealthy farmer. As a wedding gift, John Shelton gave the couple 600 acres (242 hectares) of land. Though Henry had never farmed before, he threw himself into the task of working the land. Unfortunately, it was a bad year for farmers throughout Virginia. A drought in the summer and an early frost in the fall caused Henry's tobacco crop to fail miserably. The next year, fire destroyed his house.

John Shelton took pity on the young couple, who by now had their first child. He arranged for them to move into the Hanover Tavern, where Henry was made barkeeper. Henry soon opened another store just outside of town. This time he was more successful. The tavern was across the street from Hanover Court House, and it attracted business from lawyers on their way to and from court. The lawyers also shopped at his store. Henry often overheard them arguing about the law, and their discussions intrigued him. Soon, he developed an interest in law. With a single-minded determination, he decided to become a lawyer in 1760.

In the eighteenth century, there were fewer requirements for becoming a lawyer than there are today. Although American law was based on British law, the necessities of the new land often required great flexibility. Everything about the American colonies was less formal. Many judges were learned laymen whose services were needed only occasionally. Frequently, legal decisions were based more on common sense than on legal precedent, or established law.

For prospective lawyers, this was good news. Instead of years of legal training, a man needed only to have a good head on his shoulders. In Virginia, law candidates needed to pass an oral examination given by a panel of attorneys. The examination would evaluate a candidate's abilities by engaging him in theoretical arguments about the law. Henry set to work studying. Since his days watching Reverend Davies, his speaking skills had improved. Now, he simply needed knowledge of the law. He paid closer attention to lawyers' conversations in the tavern. He asked many questions. Many recommended a book entitled *Institutes of the Laws of England* by Sir Edward Coke, which outlined how common law had developed in England.

In April 1760, Henry rode two days to Williamsburg to undergo his oral exam by a panel of Virginia's most respected lawyers. Though the well-respected John Randolph was put off by Henry's rough

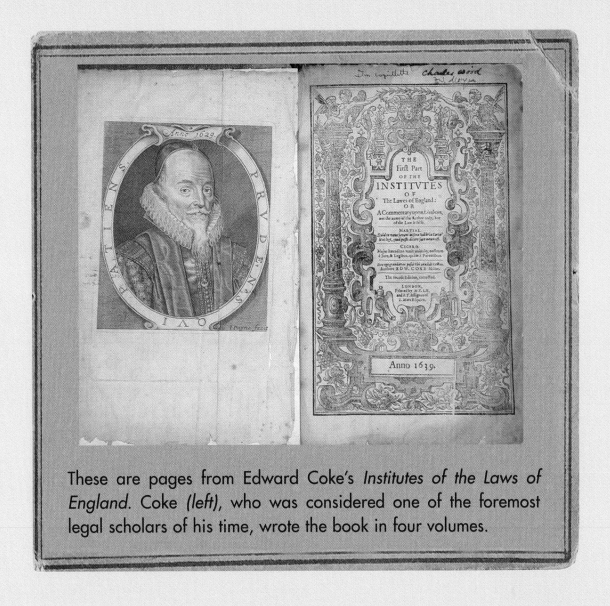

These are pages from Edward Coke's *Institutes of the Laws of England*. Coke *(left)*, who was considered one of the foremost legal scholars of his time, wrote the book in four volumes.

appearance, he was won over by his debating skills. Having passed the examination, Henry became a lawyer. He rode from county to county to present his certification. Gradually, he built up a list of clients. For the next three years, Henry went from courthouse to courthouse. He dealt with credit cases. He wrote wills. Though the cases were small, he quickly built a reputation as a man of the people. Henry spoke in a way that was simultaneously elegant and understandable.

In 1763, Henry argued in the so-called Parson's Cause case, which made him famous. Henry represented local farmers and officials. They were sued by members of the English clergy in Virginia to recover back

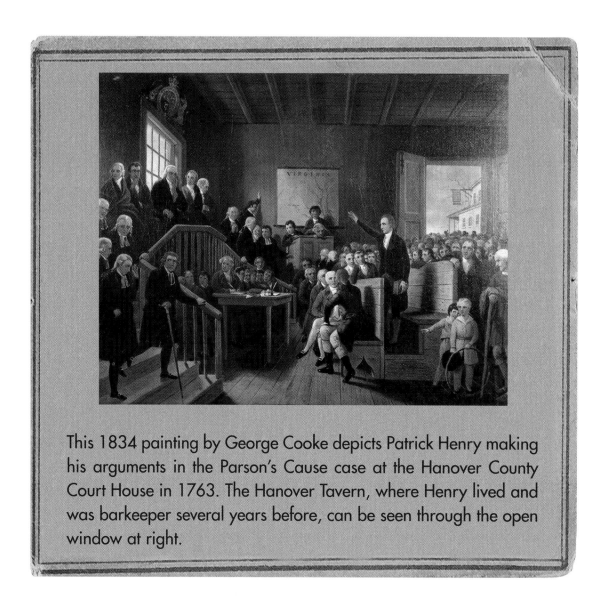

This 1834 painting by George Cooke depicts Patrick Henry making his arguments in the Parson's Cause case at the Hanover County Court House in 1763. The Hanover Tavern, where Henry lived and was barkeeper several years before, can be seen through the open window at right.

pay after King George II overturned the Two Penny Act. Before the Two Penny Act was passed, the clergy was paid in tobacco. The law had allowed locals to pay the clergy with money, but at a rate that was lower than the market price of tobacco. Henry argued passionately in court, unleashing his full powers. During his final argument, he let loose with a wildly breathless torrent of words. He declared that the king of England had "degenerated into a tyrant." The audience went mad. It stood cheering. The judge pounded his gavel to little avail. When order was restored, he ruled in favor of Henry's clients. Farmers carried Henry out of the courtroom on their shoulders in celebration.

+≈— **CHAPTER 2** ≈+

THE TAXMAN COMETH

The boisterous reception to Henry's courtroom out-burst about the king of England was a reflection of a developing rift between England and its American colonies. Over the years, the physical distance between England and the colonies, as well as the differences in the structure, pace, and opportunities of the two societies, resulted in a gradual weakening of the ties between them. Moreover, as the colonies grew, their economies thrived. Meanwhile, for various reasons, England's economy was declining. It was a peculiar relationship for a colony and a mother country to be in. The colonies were no longer dependent on England, and consequently, the power structure in the colonies began to erode. Many colonists, regardless of wealth, were gaining a feeling of independence, both at home and from England. At the same time, many members of the British parliament were concerned that the colonies were operating too freely and that they needed to be reined in.

Regulating the Colonies

Throughout much of the eighteenth century, England was engaged in a series of military conflicts known as the

Imperial Wars. These wars were fought primarily among England, Spain, and France to gain or hold territories in the Americas. The last of these wars was the French and Indian War (1754–1763). Waged between England and France for control of the Ohio territory, the war lasted nine years and took place entirely in North America. England fared well in the Imperial Wars, and the British Empire grew as a result. However, its success came at a high price. By the end of the hostilities in 1763, England was deeply in debt.

At the conclusion of the French and Indian War, England turned its attention to exercising tighter control over its colonies and reducing its debt. To meet these goals, it made a number of decisions that were resisted by the American colonists. First, with the Proclamation of 1763, King George III tried to alleviate hostilities between the colonists and American Indians by prohibiting the colonists from moving westward into territory still populated by the Indians. Next, the British parliament decided to place a large permanent army throughout its empire and to institute new taxes on the colonies to pay for it. The army was to consist of twenty regiments, each made up of approximately 1,000 soldiers.

Colonial Resistance

As angered as the colonists were by these actions, it was a series of laws passed by Parliament in 1764 and 1765 that spurred the independence movement leading to the American Revolution. The Sugar Act of 1764 lowered the existing tax on sugar products, but established strict procedures to make sure that the taxes were collected. The Currency Act of 1764 banned the issuing of colonial currency. The Stamp Act of 1765 placed a tax on many paper goods, including commercial and legal documents. Finally, the Quartering Act required colonists to provide

The Stamp Act of 1765 *(left)* was intended to tax a wide range of paper goods ranging from court and business documents to college degrees, newspapers, playing cards, and almanacs. The colonists argued that the law placed a burden on the colonies. King George III of England *(right)* stubbornly ignored the colonists' complaints. His insensitivity to their concerns led many colonists to question their allegiance to the British Crown.

housing and various household necessities for members of the permanent army.

The reaction to these laws—to the Stamp Act in particular—was explosive. Individuals regarded the new laws as attempts to weaken their personal liberties. Businessmen saw them as affronts to their financial liberties, as well as obstructions to trade. Colonists from all walks of life worked to block the implementation of the new laws and eventually overturn them. Ordinary citizens protested in the streets and in government buildings. Some activists even shut down colonial

This special edition of the *Pennsylvania Journal and Weekly Advertiser*, published on October 31, 1765, was filled with articles and cartoons protesting the Stamp Act. Editors and printers were angry that the new law taxed newspapers and pamphlets. Understandably, newspapers took the lead in criticizing King George and the British parliament.

courts to prevent the use of certain stamps. Merchants and consumers boycotted English goods. Colonial legislatures passed resolutions denouncing the laws and establishing obstacles to the collection of the taxes. In addition, political, religious, and business leaders began debating whether the laws violated the British Constitution.

A Most Vocal Rebel

Patrick Henry witnessed much of this firsthand. His rounds took him from county to county, where he saw the resistance. He could see that the colonists were developing a new identity that emphasized their American culture over their legal status as British subjects. Certain words began to cross the lips of these new Americans: Freedom. Liberty.

Many of the leaders of the American resistance were wealthy businessmen. While surely they believed in personal freedoms, much of their anger was fueled by money. In the next years, they worked to mobilize the lower classes toward revolution.

Nowhere was this better embodied than in Virginia's House of Burgesses (the colony's house of representatives), which Henry joined in 1765. It was made up predominantly of wealthy Virginians. Henry was neither rich nor experienced. He was admitted to the House of Burgesses mostly based on the fame of his speech in the Parson's Cause case. As a member of the House of Burgesses, he played a role in many of the important issues of the day.

Henry arrived for his first session on May 20, 1765, when the Stamp Act was the hot topic throughout the colonies. But nobody would raise the issue for discussion during the official proceedings of the House. It was too controversial. The governor had threatened to dissolve the House if any member even brought it up. Instead, members met to discuss the Stamp Act in taverns and hotels. Wisely, they waited for the last day of the session to discuss it on the floor of the House. They wished to lodge an official complaint against the British government. Several members wrote a resolution. Impressed by Henry's eloquence, they asked him to speak for them in the House. He agreed.

Henry's speech was aggressive. As with the Parson's Cause, he voiced what many had been thinking, but few had the courage to say. As in other political bodies, arguments in the House of Burgesses frequently rested on a knowledge of history. In speeches, members would cite legal precedents and obscure sources. Henry had none of

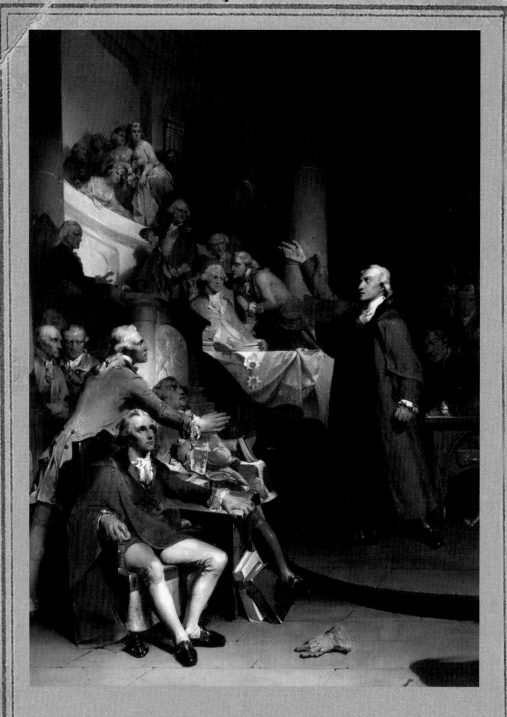

This painting portrays Patrick Henry speaking out against the Stamp Act in the Virginia House of Burgesses in 1765. Although most of his colleagues agreed with much of the sentiments he expressed, they shouted him down when he suggested that King George should be assassinated.

that. He said simply that he believed that a good American would stand up against tyranny. At the word "tyranny," John Robinson, the Speaker of the House who oversaw the proceedings, bristled. "Treason!" he shouted. "Treason!"

The resolution didn't pass. It was too strongly worded. But it was a close vote—so close that it was misreported in several places to have passed. Several Virginia newspapers printed the entire resolution. Word spread around the colonies. Many people were inspired by Henry's inflammatory remarks.

Increasing Tensions

In October, representatives from nine colonies met in New York for the Stamp Act Congress. They approved a set of fourteen resolutions, which were sent to England, protesting the Stamp Act on constitutional grounds. They argued that under the British Constitution, the colonists, as British subjects, could be taxed only by their elected representatives. Accordingly, because the colonies were not represented in Parliament, it lacked the power to tax them.

The following year, Parliament repealed the Stamp Act. This was more in response to the colonists' boycott of British goods than to their constitutional arguments. In fact, Parliament passed the Declaratory Act of 1766, reasserting its authority to make laws to regulate the colonies in all matters. It also punished New York's legislative body for violating the Quartering Act by taking away its right to pass legislation.

In the next years, tension increased dramatically between England and the American colonies. In 1767, Parliament imposed a new set of taxes on the colonies with the Townshend Revenue Act. Again, the colonies resisted the new act. By the late 1760s, the new taxes were bringing in increasingly higher revenue. However, it did little to offset the costs of keeping a standing army in the colonies. Riots and protests broke out with some consistency, to which Parliament often responded by strengthening its forces in the trouble spots. In 1770, British soldiers shot and killed several Boston citizens who had pelted them with snowballs during a protest against the Quartering Act. The incident, which became known as the Boston Massacre, further inflamed anti-British sentiment among the colonists.

By this time a familiar pattern had developed in the relationship between England and the colonies. The colonies responded to British attempts to regulate them with organized opposition. This in turn led England to punish the offending colonies by taking away some of their legislative rights or stationing more troops there. The breaking point came in 1774, in the wake of the Boston Tea Party, during which Boston residents dumped 90,000 pounds (40,823 kilograms) of tea, belonging to the British East India Company, into Boston Harbor. They were protesting against the newly instituted Tea Act, which gave the company a monopoly on the sale of tea in the colonies.

In response, Parliament passed the Coercive Acts—the Intolerable Acts, to the colonists—to punish Massachusetts. The laws closed Boston Harbor, declared that British troops could be housed in private homes, took back the Boston colonists' right to select its legislators, and authorized the Massachusetts royal governor to send officials and soldiers accused of crimes outside of the colony to be tried. All across the colonies, people were outraged. The other colonies rallied in support of Massachusetts.

In September 1774, the First Continental Congress convened in Philadelphia. Henry made the long journey from Virginia. Although the delegates did not pass a motion for independence—they were one

The Boston Massacre is sensationally portrayed in this engraving by Paul Revere. It shows a group of soldiers firing into a crowd of civilians. The first two lines of the poem below the artwork read, "Unhappy Boston! See thy Sons deplore, Thy Hallowed Walks besmeared with guiltless Gore."

vote short—the congress was still an important step. The colonies were beginning to unite. Political pamphlets circulated through the cities. They expressed a powerful anger against the British Crown. But they also expressed a strong sense of optimism. They resounded with ideas about how the Americans might better govern themselves.

Over the next several months, the colonies sent various petitions to England. These were mostly dismissed. By early 1775, it was clear that the British army was preparing for battle.

CHAPTER 3

"GIVE ME LIBERTY OR GIVE ME DEATH"

During the last months of 1774, several colonies began to hold conventions to debate how to deal with Britain's willingness to use its military might to force its policies on the colonies. Publicly, some colonial leaders joked how they would relieve the British government of the need to maintain an army, thereby saving it some money. Privately, the colonists were worried about the British army. They wanted a way to defend themselves.

Developing a Defense Strategy

In December, Maryland established a militia, a local army. A typical militia was comprised of a colony's free male inhabitants between the ages of sixteen and fifty. Militiamen armed themselves and met regularly to practice. Marylanders wanted their militia to be ready for any emergency. Henry followed these activities with great interest. He believed that Virginia, too, needed a militia.

Other high-powered Virginians agreed with him. In January 1775, George Washington and George Mason

George Washington *(left)* was already an experienced military leader by the time the colonies started creating militias to resist British rule. He was second in command of the Virginia armed forces, which fought for England during the French and Indian War. Several months after organizing the Fairfax County militia, Washington was selected to lead the Continental army. His commission *(right)* named him "Commander in Chief of the army of the United Colonies."

began to organize a militia in Fairfax County, Virginia. They suggested that a local tax might be used to pay for it. They boldly and mockingly asked the sheriff to collect it for them, even though the sheriff was an appointee of Virginia's royal governor. Henry took pleasure in this mockery of British colonial offices. He corresponded with leading dissenters in other colonies. He received news from Connecticut that militias were being organized all over New England. Many of their members had renounced their royal governors.

As a traveling lawyer, Henry was in touch with residents in the far reaches of Virginia. He began to hear from friends and clients in the

Lord Dunmore (born John Murray) was the royal governor of Virginia between 1771 and 1775. Before he fell out of favor with Virginians, he was celebrated for leading colonial forces in a successful war against the Shawnee Indians in Kentucky in 1774.

backcountry. They, too, believed that organizing a militia was a grand idea. While the backcountry was wild and occasionally lawless, it certainly produced a resilient breed of men. By necessity, the frontiersmen were well trained with rifles. They knew the land. This would become an important advantage once the war began. Henry received letters from people across the state. If Virginia were to form a militia, they pledged they would send men.

The Second Virginia Convention

The issue of public security was expected to be the topic of discussion when the House of Burgesses convened in 1775. Lord Dunmore, Virginia's royal governor, knew this. He was losing power, so he postponed calling the House of Burgesses into session. He pushed its meeting off until May. Peyton Randolph, the Speaker of the House of Burgesses who had helped to give Henry his lawyer's examination several years earlier, requested that the representatives meet in Richmond in late March to avoid interference from the royal governor and British troops. Although Henry, whose wife had died in February, was quite depressed, he traveled to Richmond.

Richmond was a small trading town. It was located on the James River. Businesses lined several streets near the waterfront. Behind them lay a steep hill. Houses were tucked into the steep grade. From the top of the slope, the view was astonishing. There, the delegates to the Virginia Convention met at the Henrico Parish Church. It was the only building in the town big enough to hold the 100 men who had traveled to Richmond.

Henry knew most of them. He had served with many of them in the House of Burgesses. Ten years before, he had argued against the Stamp Act with them. Travelers came from the far western reaches of the state, and Henry knew many of them, too.

The raucous mood was both belligerent (warlike) and optimistic. Adam Stephen, George Washington's former second in command in the army, bragged about what he would do if he met the royal governor. Rumors circulated about the business of the convention. Many thought that the convention should create its own provisional government. They wanted to levy (impose) taxes. None of the other states had gone that far. But, then, the time may have been right for such a move. Many thought that the king would punish them regardless of what they did. The petitions they had sent to England airing their grievances had done no good. They might as well go all the way and create their own government.

On the third day, Henry finally spoke. He sidestepped the issue of creating a government by proposing that the convention simply take it upon itself to organize a militia. "A well-regulated Militia composed of Gentlemen and Yeoman is the natural Strength and only Security of a free Government," his proposal read.

This 1915 painting by Clyde D. DeLand captures the passion with which Patrick Henry is reported to have given his Liberty or Death speech. One eyewitness account of the event offered that Henry's face became so pale and his eyes so glaring that he became "terrible to look on."

The debate began immediately. A lot of the delegates believed that Henry's proposal was going too far. For various reasons, they disagreed with Henry's push to go to war with England. Some were simply not as distrustful of the king as Henry was, and they believed that armed resistance was not necessary. They described Henry's proposal as being desperate. Others continued to hope for peace, arguing that, given more time, America's friends in Parliament could eventually reverse the policies. Others still were afraid to become entangled in a war in which they were sure that the British would crush the colonies.

THE MILITIA MOVEMENT

Militias still exist in the United States. The framers of the Constitution were careful to allow for them. The Bill of Rights states, "A well regulated militia, being necessary to the security of a free State, the right of the people to keep and bear Arms, shall not be infringed." The writers of the Constitution did not want the government to become too powerful.

Throughout the country, there are many people who believe today that the government is just that. In 1939, though, the U.S. Supreme Court defined "militias" as the National Guards maintained by individual states.

In recent years, gun control laws have been put in place. These laws require gun shop owners to give background checks to those buying guns. The checks make sure that the purchasers have no history of crime or mental instability. Members of militias argue that this violates the Second Amendment of the Constitution. It is a complicated issue. They claim that they might be prevented from buying a gun simply because the government is too powerful.

Edmund Pendleton, the delegate from Caroline County, said: "We must arm, you say; but gentlemen must remember that blows are apt to follow the arming, and blood will follow blows, and sir, when this occurs the dogs of war will be loosed, friends will be converted into enemies, and this flourishing country will be swept with a tornado of death and destruction."

After a while, Henry rose to defend his motion. He strode to the front of the room and began the speech he is most remembered for. He began calmly. His hands moved slightly. As he went, he built speed. His hands moved in broader gestures. His voice rose. As usual, Henry appealed to his audience by being personal. "I have but one lamp by which my feet are guided," he explained, "and that is the lamp of experience." As Henry gained steam, his speech moved from the politeness of a politician to the passion of a preacher.

CHAPTER 4

THE MEANING OF HENRY'S SPEECH

H enry began his speech by telling his colleagues that he intended to be brutally honest and that he hoped no one would take offense at his arguments. In so doing, Henry was acknowledging his reputation as a radical politician who many, including some of his supporters, thought sometimes crossed the line between spirited debate and reckless flame-throwing. Perhaps he did not want that reputation to get in the way of what he regarded as his legitimate proposal to take the extreme step of preparing for war with England. More important, he believed that the matter they were discussing was too significant to simply whitewash the truth.

> This is no time for ceremony. The question before the house is one of awful moment to this country. For my own part, I consider it as nothing less than a question of freedom or slavery; and in proportion to the magnitude of the subject ought to be the freedom of the debate. It is only in this way that we can hope to arrive at the truth, and fulfill the great responsibility

which we hold to God and our country. Should I keep back my opinions at such a time, through fear of giving offense, I should consider myself as guilty of treason towards my country, and of an act of disloyalty toward the Majesty of Heaven, which I revere above all earthly kings.

This passage unveils several themes that are borne out in the rest of the speech. First, Henry likened the relationship between England and the colonies to slavery. This certainly echoed the sentiments of the colonists, who bristled at the British threat and use of force to impose policies in which they had no say. Further in the speech, Henry said, "Our chains are forged! Their clanging may be heard on the plains of Boston!" The slavery comparison is even more striking because slavery was legal and widely practiced in the colonies. But Henry, who himself owned slaves, regarded it as a moral wrong. In a January 18, 1773, letter to Quaker leader Robert Pleasants, he had described slavery as a "lamentable evil" that he hoped would soon be abolished.

Second, Henry used the terms "our country" and "my country" in referring to Virginia, in particular, and all the colonies in general. This clearly reflected the American identity that the colonists developed over time, especially in the years since Britain sought to tighten its control over them. As a result, Henry, like many of the colonists, found it easy to speak of a patriotism that was limited to the colonies and of treason that ignored the concerns of England.

Third, the passage, as does the rest of the speech, has a strong religious tone. This is in part a reflection of the influence of the revivalist preachers from Henry's youth. Also, it was common practice among public speakers of the time to invoke God to add credibility to their declarations. Moreover, there was a developing notion within the colonies that God had a special purpose for them. Henry later emphasized this notion when he declared, "There is a just God who presides over the destinies of nations, and who will raise up friends to fight our battles for us." He saw war with England not only as a patriotic act but also as a religious duty.

A Call to War

Henry then set about framing "the awful moment" that the colonies faced. He encouraged his colleagues to not give way to a false hope that the quarrel with England could be settled peacefully. For Henry, it was not an option to do nothing with the hope that things would somehow get better, especially when the actions of Great Britain over the previous ten years suggested that it intended to force the colonies into submission. Using a series of pointed rhetorical questions, Henry drove home his point.

> Are fleets and armies necessary to a work of love and reconciliation? Have we shown ourselves so unwilling to be reconciled that force must be called in to win back our love? Let us not deceive ourselves, sir. These are the implements of war and subjugation; the last arguments to which kings resort. I ask gentlemen, sir, what means this martial array, if its purpose be not to force us to submission? Can gentlemen assign any other possible motive for it? Has Great Britain any enemy, in this quarter of the world, to call for all this accumulation of navies and armies? No, sir, she has none. They are meant for us: they can be meant for no other.

Henry also made it clear that the time for talking was over. He didn't see the value of continuing to reach out to England, when King George

By his Excellency the Right Hon. JOHN Earl of DUNMORE, his Majesty's Lieutenant and Governor General of the Colony and Dominion of VIRGINIA, and Vice Admiral of the same:

A Proclamation.

VIRGINIA, to wit,

WHEREAS I have been informed, from undoubted Authority, that a certain *Patrick Henry*, of the County of *Hanover*, and a Number of deluded Followers, have taken up Arms, chosen their Officers, and styling themselves an Independent Company, have marched out of their County, encamped, and put themselves in a Posture of War; and have written and dispatched Letters to divers Parts of the Country, exciting the People to join in these outrageous and rebellious Practices, to the great Terrour of all his Majesty's faithful Subjects, and in open Defiance of Law and Government; and have committed other Acts of Violence, particularly in extorting from his Majesty's Receiver General the Sum of £. 330, under Pretence of replacing the Powder I thought proper to order from the Magazine; whence it undeniably appears, that there is no longer the least Security for the Life or Property of any Man: WHEREFORE I have thought proper, with the Advice of his Majesty's Council, and in his Majesty's Name, to issue this my Proclamation, strictly charging all Persons, upon their Allegiance, not to aid, abet, or give Countenance to, the said *Patrick Henry*, or any other Persons concerned in such unwarrantable Combinations; but, on the Contrary, to oppose them and their Designs by every Means; which Designs must, otherwise, inevitably involve the whole Country in the most direful Calamity, as they will call for the Vengeance of offended Majesty and the insulted Laws, to be exerted here, to vindicate the constitutional Authority of Government.

GIVEN under my Hand, and the Seal of the Colony, at Williamsburg, this 6th Day of May, 1775, and in the 15th Year of his Majesty's Reign.

DUNMORE.

GOD SAVE THE KING.

Lord Dunmore issued this proclamation in which he named Patrick Henry a wanted criminal shortly after Henry delivered his Liberty or Death speech in 1775. However, Dunmore had pretty much lost control of Virginia by this time. By the end of the year, Dunmore fled from Virginia after having lost an armed battle against Virginia militias.

and Parliament were not receptive to the colonists' arguments. It was time for action.

> There is no longer any room for hope. If we wish to be free . . . we must fight! . . . An appeal to arms and to the God of hosts is all that is left us! They tell us, sir, that we are weak; unable to cope with so formidable an adversary. But when shall we be stronger? Will it be the next week, or the next year? Will it be when we are totally disarmed, and when a British guard shall be stationed in every house? . . . Sir, we are not weak if we make a proper use of those means which the God of nature hath placed in our power. The millions of people, armed in the holy cause of liberty, and in such a country as that which we possess, are invincible by any force which our enemy can send against us.

Here, too, Henry addressed those representatives who feared going to war because they believed the colonies were no match for Britain's military power. He acknowledged the mismatch but felt that, with right and God on their side, the colonies could channel their anger and use their numbers and knowledge of the land to face down the British troops. He also felt that delaying action would only make the task harder. "There is no retreat, but in submission and slavery," he said.

In a masterful turn, Henry posed the most effective rhetorical question of his speech. "Is life so dear, or peace so sweet, as to be purchased at the price of chains and slavery?" It was a question that had only one reasonable or desirable answer. It need not have been answered, but Henry left no room for doubt. "Forbid it, Almighty God! I know not what course others may take; but as for me, give me liberty or give me death."

The Immediate Reaction

Reports from the meeting said that as Henry delivered this famous closing line, he motioned as if driving a dagger into his heart. There was a stunned silence in the church. Henry had framed the most political issues in an intensely personal way. The silence lasted for several minutes. Debate soon resumed, but it was merely a formality. Henry's resolution passed by five votes. Henry was named the head of the militia committee. He and others, including Thomas Jefferson, had already concocted a plan. They submitted it to the convention the next morning.

Although Henry's language called down the gods, he spoke as an individual. His was the voice of the people. Around the colonies, other voices were being raised with similar arguments, and other conventions were coming to the same conclusion of the Virginia Convention. Four weeks later, independent of such decisions, the war began in Massachusetts.

CHAPTER 5

THE AMERICAN REVOLUTION

In mid-April, colonists in Boston received word that the British army was planning to seize some of the colonists' weapons and ammunition from a storehouse in Concord, Massachusetts. Paul Revere rode ahead of the British soldiers. He warned local leaders John Hancock and Samuel Adams to flee. He also roused the local militia, known as the minutemen. The farmers of Concord gathered their weapons. They stood against the redcoats on the town green at Lexington. Nobody knows who fired first, but it soon became known as "the shot heard 'round the world." The American Revolution had begun.

Henry's words echoed across the land. "Give me liberty or give me death" became a rallying cry for men and women across the colonies. It was a powerful slogan that bridged two elements in society. For farmers and common citizens, it was a call to arms. It contained the pure conviction of being willing to die for one's beliefs. These were the men who would actually fight the Revolution. Many sewed the motto onto their ragged militia uniforms.

For politicians and scholars, it placed the focus on the meaning of liberty. "Liberty" is a vague term, but it was what

This illustration portrays the Battle of Lexington, which took place on April 19, 1775. It was the first battle of the American Revolution. The Battle of Lexington was over within half an hour. Eight colonists were killed in the battle. The illustration was engraved by Amos Doolittle based on eyewitness accounts.

they would be fighting for. There would be many intellectual battles about what, exactly, the word "liberty" meant. Around the colonies, new local governments were springing up, openly defying British rule. Henry's phrase became the intellectual and moral fuel behind the revolutionary fire.

More and more frequently, the new local governments were comprised of regular workingmen. Politically, a new emphasis was placed on the individual or the common man. In this, an important shift in thinking occurred. Government did not grant liberty to its citizens. Liberty was inherent in the individual. Government's role, then, was to

This flag was carried by Virginia's Culpepper County militia during the American Revolution. It bears the slogan "Liberty or Death" from Patrick Henry's speech. It also includes a picture of a rattlesnake with thirteen rattles—one for each colony—and a warning that states "Don't tread on me."

balance control in respect to the rights and liberties of its citizens. It was to serve the people, not the other way around. The idea that regular men should control the government was truly revolutionary. It shocked the British.

Throughout the colonies, local governments expressed this in varying ways. Some governments forwarded the idea of the secret ballot to maintain citizens' privacy. (Before that, much voting was done by a simple show of hands.) Many opened legislative meetings to the public. Likewise, many people now demanded public reporting of government business, such as publishing the minutes of meetings. Some demanded a public record of how their representatives voted.

Another shift occurred in the spread of information. Politicians once derived much of their knowledge by studying the great works of political philosophers such as John Locke and Niccolò Machiavelli. In the colonies, it became popular to distribute pamphlets. During 1775 and 1776, the colonies were flooded with hundreds of them. Printing was cheap. Anybody who wanted to spread his ideas could do so, and many did.

The most popular pamphlet was *Common Sense*, written by Thomas Paine. The ideas contained within it were not new. But they were ideas that few had spoken. Like Henry, Paine made what had once been information for intellectuals into something accessible to the people. Political pamphlets had often used Latin phrases to make

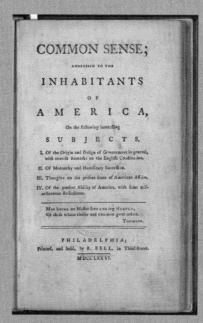

Thomas Paine *(left)* was a resident of the colonies for a little more than a year when he wrote the pamphlet *Common Sense (right)* in January 1776. Nevertheless, he became one of the most influential voices of the American Revolution. Not only did he urge independence, but he also suggested that the colonies break all ties with England.

their ideas sound important. Paine used everyday language. He called King George a "royal brute." He quoted books everybody knew, such as the Bible. *Common Sense* became a popular discussion topic in taverns. More than 120,000 copies sold in less than three months. Paine showed that all that mattered in politics was the ability for one to think for oneself. A person didn't need to know the entire history of the world to know what was right for him.

In the late spring of 1776, the Second Continental Congress met in Philadelphia. There, Thomas Jefferson created a political document that articulated the unrest throughout the colonies. It was the Declaration of Independence. In 1,300 words, Jefferson framed these new thoughts of common liberty into a more formal political language. "We hold these truths to be self-evident, that all men are created equal," he wrote. Again, it was written from the perspective of the common man, as opposed to the government that looked over him.

Meanwhile, the war raged on. With Henry's saying, the Declaration of Independence, and the idea of liberty at their backs, George Washington and the Continental army pressed on. It was tough going. They suffered many setbacks. The British redcoats had an entire empire behind them. They were well trained and had ample supplies. Washington and his men were often working on the brink of starvation. "These are the times that try men's souls," Thomas Paine wrote.

Several times, Washington was almost forced to surrender, but he and his army pressed on. The war reinforced the philosophical belief that the common man was just as good as the intellectual. Though the redcoats and their generals were professionally trained, they were not familiar with the American terrain. Militias from all over the colonies joined Washington's Continental army. Although his men were ragged, they knew the land. They had no problem hiding in bushes or scattering chaotically when needed.

The months stretched into years, with each side making numerous gains and beating hasty retreats. By 1780, the American army was on its last legs. Washington faced several mutinies. Soon, though, the Americans received military aide from the French navy. Throughout 1781, the Continental army won several decisive victories in the south. In October, British general Charles Cornwallis surrendered to Washington at Yorktown, Virginia. The American Revolution was over. The Americans had won.

The time had now come for self-government. The Articles of Confederation was the first American attempt to embody liberty in a system of government. It established the United States as a confederacy.

IN CONGRESS, JULY 4, 1776.

A DECLARATION

BY THE REPRESENTATIVES OF THE

UNITED STATES OF AMERICA,

IN GENERAL CONGRESS ASSEMBLED.

This is the surviving fragment of the original printing of the Declaration of Independence. John Hancock, president of the Continental Congress, sent it to General George Washington on July 6, 1776. Washington ordered the Declaration of Independence to be read to his troops in New York three days later.

THE MIGHTY PAMPHLETEERS

Thomas Paine's *Common Sense* was but one of many pamphlets. The American colonies were flooded with them during the years leading up to the revolution. Pamphlets had much appeal to rebellious thinkers. They differed from magazines and newspapers in that they were issued as sole publications. There was never a next issue. This meant that authors could easily remain anonymous. (*Common Sense* originally appeared without a credited author.) Therefore, the government could never retaliate against the writer.

Also, because they weren't regular publications, there was no advertising in pamphlets. Authors did not have to worry about finding sponsors, nor did they have to worry about offending them. The result was that the authors were allowed to write freely. Pamphlets were often filled with truly fringe ideas. Authors were frequently profane and openly rebellious. Pamphlets were a democratic way to get extreme opinions into the public eye.

Pamphlets proved to be a durable and lasting medium. Political and religious pamphlets were widespread in American society until well into the twentieth century. They accompanied every major political movement. Even more than newspapers, the range of published pamphlets reflected the broad range of American opinion.

The writers of the articles wanted liberty to be accounted for at every level. Thus, each state would remain sovereign (independent) from the others. The central government would have no power to tax the populace. In fact, its only function would be to provide for the nation's defense. The writers of the articles were so scared of the central government having too much power that they made it virtually powerless. The result was a continuation of the political chaos that had filled the colonies during war. Each state had its own currency, and banks and creditors printed their own money. The economic affairs of the fledgling United States were a mess.

Each state even had to negotiate its own treaties with foreign nations. Likewise, each had to negotiate with the local American Indian tribes. Though the central government had the right to do so, it couldn't muster up an army without tax revenues. The result was madness. This state of affairs left the country vulnerable to attack. For the moment, the grand experiment seemed to be failing. There was freedom. There was liberty. But was there too much?

CHAPTER 6

THE FIGHT FOR RATIFICATION

In early 1787, plans were made to hold the Constitutional Convention in Philadelphia to amend the Articles of Confederation. Most knew that this meant granting more power to a central government. No one knew to what extent.

In May 1787, fifty-five men descended on the Pennsylvania city and set to work. The men were predominantly upper class and almost universally well educated. They represented a small portion of American society and attempted to create a document that was capable of governing all.

James Madison presented the first proposal. It was known as the Virginia Plan. Under it, the United States would be reformed in a radical way. It would no longer be a confederacy of states. Rather, it would be a unified republic. Just as counties made up states, states would make up the nation. It would create an organized hierarchy of power. This was too much for some. The New Jersey Plan offered a counterproposal that favored states' rights. It granted more power to the federal government, but each state would essentially remain an independent entity.

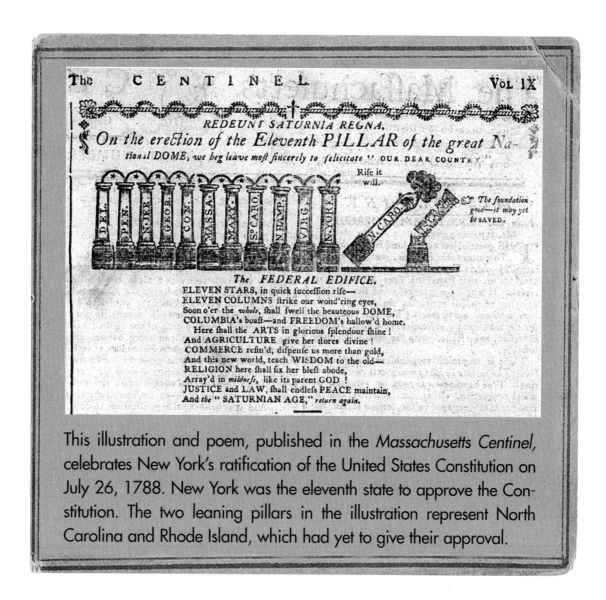

The CENTINEL. Vol. IX

REDEUNT SATURNIA REGNA.

On the erection of the Eleventh PILLAR of the great National DOME, we beg leave most sincerely to felicitate "OUR DEAR COUNTRY."

Rise it will.

The foundation good—it may yet be SAVED.

The FEDERAL EDIFICE.

ELEVEN STARS, in quick succession rise—
ELEVEN COLUMNS strike our wond'ring eyes,
Soon o'er the *whole*, shall swell the beauteous DOME,
COLUMBIA's boast—and FREEDOM's hallow'd home.
Here shall the ARTS in glorious splendour shine!
And AGRICULTURE give her stores divine!
COMMERCE refin'd; dispense us more than gold,
And this new world, teach WISDOM to the old—
RELIGION here shall fix her blest abode,
Array'd in *mildness*, like its parent GOD!
JUSTICE and LAW, shall endless PEACE maintain,
And the "SATURNIAN AGE," *return again.*

This illustration and poem, published in the *Massachusetts Centinel,* celebrates New York's ratification of the United States Constitution on July 26, 1788. New York was the eleventh state to approve the Constitution. The two leaning pillars in the illustration represent North Carolina and Rhode Island, which had yet to give their approval.

These were the terms of the debate. It raged over the summer and into early fall. Apparent stalemates were reached, and compromises were made. The resulting Constitution established three branches of federal government: the executive, legislative, and judicial. The executive branch, led by the president, would command the armed forces and control judiciary appointments. The legislative branch, comprised of Congress, would create laws. The judicial branch, led by the Supreme Court, would interpret the laws. An elaborate system of checks and balances was created, so that no branch could gain too much power.

The convention concluded in September. The Constitution had been forged. Now it had to be presented to the individual states for approval. This would prove a challenge. The Constitution was a flawed document. Voting rights were extremely limited. Only one part of the federal government, the House of Representatives, would be determined by a simple popular election. The rest would be elected through a convoluted system of state legislatures.

More troubling was the fact that, in effect, the Constitution only represented a certain portion of the populace. The Constitution didn't explicitly exclude women, slaves, American Indians, and men without property from voting. However, the state governments, led by the very men who drafted the Constitution, deprived these groups of the right to vote. In fact, despite the claim in the Declaration of Independence that "all men are created equal," women, slaves, and Indians had virtually no rights in early America. Their exclusion from the Constitution was not surprising, even to its fiercest critics. To many, though, it was particularly bothersome.

Many feared the Constitution existed to serve its creators' interests. After all, if only men with property could vote, then how would men without property be represented? Many resented this. It created a division between rich and poor, and it made the poor powerless. In fact, the Constitution itself did very little to protect the rights of its citizens.

Patrick Henry was troubled by the new Constitution. Though it began with the phrase "We the people," Henry saw little reason to believe that the Constitution was for "the people." It was for the states, he argued. Ultimately, he believed, the result would be a tyrannical government and a powerless citizenry. Even its very creation was a sign of tyranny, he claimed. The framers of the Constitution had met in Philadelphia to fix the Articles of Confederation, not create a whole

This engraving depicts George Washington addressing a group of delegates at the Constitutional Convention in Philadelphia, Pennsylvania, in 1787. The convention was a rather contentious affair. Three delegates—George Mason and Edmund Randolph of Virginia and Elbridge Gerry of Massachusetts—refused to sign the draft of the Constitution.

new government! "The people gave them no power to use their name!" he complained at the Virginia ratification convention in June 1788.

Twelve years earlier, colonies had met to form militias. Now, as states, they met to ratify (approve) the Constitution. The debate raged across the United States. Those in favor of the new plan were known as the Federalists. Those against it, such as Henry, were known as the Anti-Federalists. Alexander Hamilton, James Madison, and John Jay—some of the Constitution's creators—published an anonymous series of articles in New York newspapers. They became known as the

Federalist papers. They laid out the basic terms of the debate. Once again, Henry became the champion of the people. He was one voice out of many, but his was a loud and well-spoken one.

The Virginia ratification convention was filled with political stars. In addition to Henry, there were James Madison, Benjamin Harrison, James Monroe, Richard Henry Lee, George Mason, and others in attendance. George Washington remained at home at Mount Vernon, though he communicated with the convention daily through letters. It was clear from the outset that the debate would not be easy. Though Henry's health was declining, he remained the center of attention. His powers of rhetoric had not diminished.

The convention was filled with drama. Some high-profile politicians, such as Virginia governor Edmund Randolph, switched their positions from Federalist to Anti-Federalist. Henry declared that the Constitution lacked a basic bill of rights. While there were checks and balances in the system, they acted only between the states and the federal government. A bill of rights would protect the rights of individuals. Nobody disagreed.

Henry argued that the Constitution should be rewritten. His opponents argued that it should be ratified and amended later. Henry didn't see the point. To approve an arrangement, then specify the details seemed illogical to him. The debate continued. Both Henry and his opponents introduced items they wished to see included in a bill of rights. They soon voted on whether to ratify the Constitution. The results were 89–79 in favor of the Constitution. However, the delegates also passed a declaration of rights, predominantly penned by Henry. It included the right to free speech and the right to bear arms, and it prevented the government from forcing citizens to house soldiers in their homes.

These articles were adopted during the first session of the U.S. Congress. They became the basis for the first ten amendments to the Constitution. They are a testament to the power of Patrick Henry.

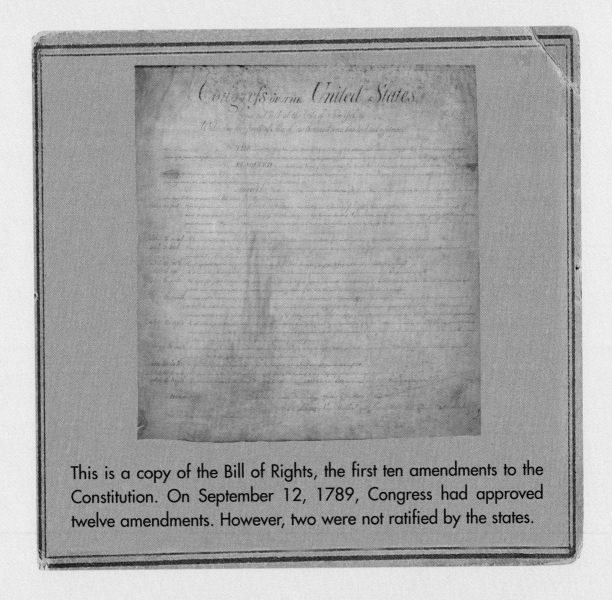

This is a copy of the Bill of Rights, the first ten amendments to the Constitution. On September 12, 1789, Congress had approved twelve amendments. However, two were not ratified by the states.

Though he was not the sole architect of the Bill of Rights by any means, he was the main force behind its rapid adoption.

Thus, his legacy remains as a man of liberty. Though the Constitution defines the United States government, it is perhaps the Bill of Rights that defines the people. Henry believed that liberty grew from individuals, and he worked to allow people to understand that. It was never said more elegantly: "Give me liberty or give me death." He was given liberty. But, more important, he gave liberty and did his best to ensure that every American would have it every day.

"Give Me Liberty or Give Me Death"

No man thinks more highly than I do of the patriotism, as well as abilities, of the very worthy gentlemen who have just addressed the house. But different men often see the same subject in different lights; and, therefore, I hope it will not be thought disrespectful to those gentlemen if, entertaining as I do opinions of a character very opposite to theirs, I shall speak forth my sentiments freely and without reserve. This is no time for ceremony. The question before the house is one of awful moment to this country. For my own part, I consider it as nothing less than a question of freedom or slavery; and in proportion to the magnitude of the subject ought to be the freedom of the debate. It is only in this way that we can hope to arrive at the truth, and fulfill the great responsibility which we hold to God and our country. Should I keep back my opinions at such a time, through fear of giving offense, I should consider myself as guilty of treason towards my country, and of an act of disloyalty toward the Majesty of Heaven, which I revere above all earthly kings.

Mr. President, it is natural to man to indulge in the illusions of hope. We are apt to shut our eyes against a painful truth, and listen to the song of that siren till she transforms us into beasts. Is this the part of wise men, engaged in a great and arduous struggle for liberty? Are we disposed to be of the numbers of those who, having eyes, see not, and, having ears, hear not, the things which so nearly concern their temporal salvation? For my part, whatever anguish of spirit it may cost, I am willing to know the whole truth, to know the worst, and to provide for it.

I have but one lamp by which my feet are guided, and that is the lamp of experience. I know of no way of judging of the future but by the past. And judging by the past, I wish to know what there has been in the conduct of the British ministry for the last ten years to justify those hopes with which gentlemen have been pleased to solace themselves and the House. Is it that insidious smile with which our petition has been lately received?

Trust it not, sir; it will prove a snare to your feet. Suffer not yourselves to be betrayed with a kiss. Ask yourselves how this gracious reception of our petition comports with those warlike preparations which cover our waters and darken our land.

There is no longer any room for hope. If we wish to be free—if we mean to preserve inviolate those inestimable privileges for which we have been so long contending—if we mean not basely to abandon the noble struggle in which we have been so long engaged, and which we have pledged ourselves never to abandon until the glorious object of our contest shall be obtained—we must fight! I repeat it, sir, we must fight! An appeal to arms and to the God of hosts is all that is left us! They tell us, sir, that we are weak; unable to cope with so formidable an adversary. But when shall we be stronger? Will it be the next week, or the next year? Will it be when we are totally disarmed, and when a British guard shall be stationed in every house? Shall we gather strength but irresolution and inaction? Shall we acquire the means of effectual resistance by lying supinely on our backs and hugging the delusive phantom of hope, until our enemies shall have bound us hand and foot? Sir, we are not weak if we make a proper use of those means which the God of nature hath placed in our power. The millions of people, armed in the holy cause of liberty, and in such a country as that which we possess, are invincible by any force which our enemy can send against us. Besides, sir, we shall not fight our battles alone. There is a just God who presides over the destinies of nations, and who will raise up friends to fight our battles for us. The battle, sir, is not to the strong alone; it is to the vigilant, the active, the brave. Besides, sir, we have no election. If we were base enough to desire it, it is now too late to retire from the contest. There is no retreat but in submission and slavery! Our chains are forged! Their clanking may be heard on the plains of Boston! The war is inevitable—and let it come! I repeat it, sir, let it come.

It is in vain, sir, to extenuate the matter. Gentlemen may cry, Peace, Peace—but there is no peace. The war is actually begun! The next gale that sweeps from the north will bring to our ears the clash of resounding arms! Our brethren are already in the field! Why stand we here idle? What is it that gentlemen wish? What would they have? Is life so dear, or peace so sweet, as to be purchased at the price of chains and slavery? Forbid it, Almighty God! I know not what course others may take; but as for me, give me liberty or give me death!

TIMELINE

1736   Patrick Henry is born.

1745   George Whitefield travels through Hanover County, Virginia.

1760   Henry becomes a lawyer.

1763   The French and Indian War ends. Henry argues the Parson's Cause case.

1764   England passes the Sugar Act and the Currency Act.

1765   England passes the Stamp Act and the Quartering Act. Henry joins the House of Burgesses.

1766   The Declaratory Act is passed.

1770   The Boston Massacre takes place.

1773   The Boston Tea Party takes place.

1774   England passes the Coercive Acts. The First Continental Congress is convened.

1775   Henry delivers his "Give me liberty or give me death" speech at the Virginia Convention. The American Revolution begins.

1776 The Declaration of Independence is signed. Thomas Paine publishes *Common Sense*.

1781 England surrenders to the Continental army at Yorktown, Virginia. The American Revolution ends.

1787 The Constitutional Convention convenes in Philadelphia. The battle for ratification ensues.

1791 The Bill of Rights is ratified.

1799 Patrick Henry dies.

GLOSSARY

Anti-Federalist One in opposition to the Constitution and in favor of a confederate government.

apprentice A person who learns a trade by working for an experienced person.

aristocracy People of a high social or economic class.

belligerent Hostile or inclined to wage war.

confederacy A form of government comprised of smaller, mostly independent states.

Federalist One in support of the Constitution and in favor of a republican government.

itinerant Constantly traveling.

layman A person who is not a member of the clergy or a specific profession; a person who has no special knowledge of a given science or art.

militia An army comprised of private citizens.

pamphlet A small publication of limited distribution.

republic A form of government elected by individual citizens.

sovereign Independent.

tariff A tax on imported or exported goods.

tyrant One who exhibits absolute control unjustly.

FOR MORE INFORMATION

The Colonial Williamsburg Foundation
P.O. Box 1776
Williamsburg, VA 23187-1776
Web site: http://www.history.org

Independence Hall
143 South Third Street
Philadelphia, PA 19106
Web site: http://www.nps.gov/inde/
Independence Hall is now a national historic site, run by the
National Park Service.

Patrick Henry National Memorial
1250 Red Hill Road
Brookneal, VA 24528
Web site: http://www.redhill.org

Web Sites

Due to the changing nature of Internet links, the Rosen Publishing
Group, Inc., has developed an online list of Web sites related to the
subject of this book. This site is updated regularly. Please use this
link to access the list:

http://www.rosenlinks.com/ghds/phld

FOR FURTHER READING

Kukla, Jon, and Amy Kukla. *Patrick Henry: The Voice of the Revolution*. New York: PowerKids Press, 2002.

McPherson, Stephanie Sammartino. *Liberty or Death: A Story About Patrick Henry* (Creative Minds Biography). Minneapolis: Lerner Publishing Group, 2003.

Vaughan, David J., and George E Grant. *Give Me Liberty: The Uncompromising Statesmanship of Patrick Henry* (Leaders in Action Series). Nashville: Cumberland House, 1997.

Wood, Gordon S. *The American Revolution: A History*. New York: The Modern Library, 2002.

Wright, Mike. *What They Didn't Teach You About the American Revolution*. Novato, CA: Presidio Press, 1999.

BIBLIOGRAPHY

Beard, Charles A. *An Economic Interpretation of the Constitution of the United States*. New York: The Free Press, 1941.

Bowen, Catherine Drinker. *Miracle at Philadelphia: The Story of the Constitutional Convention, May to September, 1787*. Boston: Back Bay Books, 1966.

Cavallo, Dominick. *A Fiction of the Past: The Sixties in American History*. New York: Palgrave Books, 1999.

Hamilton, Alexander, John Jay, and James Madison. *The Federalist Papers*. Garry Wills, ed. New York: Bantam Books, 1982.

Inge, M. Thomas, ed. *Concise Histories of American Popular Culture*. Westport, CT: Greenwood Publishing Group, 1982.

Marston, Daniel. *The American Revolution, 1774–1783* (Essential Histories). Oxford, England: Osprey Press, 2002.

Mayer, Henry. *A Son of Thunder: Patrick Henry and the American Republic*. Charlottesville, VA: University Press of Virginia, 1991.

Wood, Gordon S. *The American Revolution: A History*. New York: The Modern Library, 2002.

Wright, Mike. *What They Didn't Teach You About the American Revolution*. Novato, CA: Presidio Press, 1999.

Zinn, Howard. *A People's History of the United States*. New York: HarperCollins, 1999.

PRIMARY SOURCE IMAGE LIST

Page 10: Portrait of Samuel Davies, after an original painting by Alexander von Jost. Housed at the Virginia Historical Society.

Page 13: *Institutes of the Laws of England*, by Edward Coke, 1639. Housed at the Boston College Law Library in Newton Centre, Massachusetts.

Page 14: *Patrick Henry Arguing the Parson's Cause at the Hanover Court House*, by George Cooke, 1834. Housed at the Virginia Historical Society.

Page 17 (left): The Stamp Act of 1765. Housed at the Library of Congress Manuscript Division in Washington, D.C.

Page 17 (right): Portrait of King George III, undated eighteenth-century illustration. Housed at the Library of Congress Prints and Photographs Division in Washington, D.C.

Page 18: The October 31, 1765, edition of the *Pennsylvania Journal and Weekly Advertiser*.

Page 23: *The Bloody Massacre Perpetrated in King Street Boston on March 5th 1770 by a Party of the 29th Regt*, created in 1770 by Paul Revere. Housed at the Library of Congress Prints and Photographs Division in Washington, D.C.

Page 26 (left): Portrait of George Washington, oil on canvas. Created between 1787 and 1790 by James Peale.

Page 26 (right): George Washington's commission as commander in chief of the American army, June 19, 1775. Housed at the Library of Congress Manuscript Division in Washington, D.C.

Page 27: Undated portrait of John Murray, Earl of Dunmore. Housed at the Virginia Historical Society in Richmond, Virginia.

Page 35: Proclamation by Lord Dunmore against Patrick Henry, 1775. Housed at the Library of Congress in Washington, D.C.

Page 39: The Battle of Lexington, 1775, engraving by Amos Doolittle.

Page 41 (left): Portrait of Thomas Paine, engraving by William Sharp, 1793. Housed at the Library of Congress Prints and Photographs Division in Washington, D.C.

Page 41 (right): *Common Sense*, pamphlet, 1776. Housed at the Library of Congress in Washington, D.C.

Page 43: Fragment from the original printing of the Declaration of Independence, 1776. Housed at the Library of Congress Manuscript Division in Washington, D.C.

Page 47: *The Federal Edifice*, illustration and poem, 1787, published in the *Massachusetts Centinel*.

Page 49: Convention at Philadelphia, 1787, engraving. Published in a *History of the United States of America* in 1823. Housed at the Library of Congress Prints and Photographs Division in Washington, D.C.

INDEX

About the Author

Jesse Jarnow is a freelance writer who lives in Brooklyn, New York.

Photo Credits

Cover (left), p. 4 (left), 26 (left) Independence National Historic Park; cover (right), pp. 4 (right), 41 (left), 49 Library of Congress Prints and Photographs Division; p. 8 © Hulton Archive/Getty Images; pp. 10, 14, 27, 40 Virginia Historical Society; p. 13 courtesy of the Boston College Law Library's Daniel R. Coquillette Rare Book Room, used by permission; pp. 17 (left), 26 (right), 43, 47 Library of Congress Manuscript Division; pp. 17 (right), 29 © Bettmann/Corbis; p. 18 © Corbis; p. 20 © Red Hill, The Patrick Henry National Memorial; p. 23 Library of Congress Rare Books and Manuscripts Division; p. 35 Library of Congress Printed Ephemera Collection, Portfolio 178, Folder 13d; p. 39 © Arthur D'Arazien/SuperStock; p. 41 (right) Library of Congress Rare Book and Special Collection Division; p. 51 National Archives and Records Administration.

Design: Les Kanturek; **Editor:** Wayne Anderson